I can ♡ cope!

I USE MINDFULNESS TO COPE

CAITIE MCANENEY

PowerKiDS
press

Published in 2023 by The Rosen Publishing Group, Inc.
2544 Clinton Street, Buffalo, NY 14224

First Edition

Book Design: Michael Flynn

Photo Credits: Cover Roman Samborskyi/Shutterstock.com; series background Abscent Vector/Shutterstock.com; p. 5 Purino/Shutterstock.com; p. 6 RimDream/Shutterstock.com; p. 7 Prostock-studio/Shutterstock.com; p. 9 Just dance/Shutterstock.com; p. 11 fizkes/Shutterstock.com; p. 12 Elena Chevalier/Shutterstock.com; p. 13 ESB Professional/Shutterstock.com; p. 15 Ami Parikh/Shutterstock.com; p. 17 Amorn Suriyan/Shutterstock.com; p. 19 Adamov_d/Shutterstock.com; p. 21 Chinnapong/Shutterstock.com.

Cataloging-in-Publication Data

Names: McAneney, Caitie.
Title: I use mindfulness to cope / by Caitie McAneney.
Description: New York : Powerkids Press, 2023. | Series: I can cope! | Includes glossary and index.
Identifiers: ISBN 9781538389515 (pbk.) | ISBN 9781538389539 (library bound) | ISBN 9781538389546 (ebook)
Subjects: LCSH: Mindfulness (Psychology)–Juvenile literature.
Classification: LCC BF637.M56 M45 2023 | DDC 158.1'3–dc23

Manufactured in the United States of America

Some of the images in this book illustrate individuals who are models. The depictions do not imply actual situations or events.

CPSIA Compliance Information: Batch #CWPK23. For Further Information contact Rosen Publishing at 1-800-237-9932.

Find us on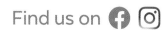

CONTENTS

♡ Dealing with Feelings

Imagine this: you're at school, but unable to **focus** on what your teacher is saying. You're thinking about a fight that happened at home that morning. You're worried about something you have to do over the weekend. Your thoughts are running wild and you start to get upset.

Thinking about the past or future can cause a lot of **stress**. Mindfulness is a coping tool, or something that helps you deal with hard feelings. Mindfulness means being aware of the present moment.

COPING TOOLBOX

♡

PRACTICING MINDFULNESS CAN HELP YOU FOCUS, DEAL WITH FEELINGS, LET GO OF STRESS, AND BOOST YOUR MEMORY.

Mindfulness means living in the "now."
Anyone can practice mindfulness and see its benefits.

♡ Stuck in the Past

We often think about things that happened in the past. You might play events over and over in your mind. You might think about them often. That's called rumination.

COPING TOOLBOX

♡

One way to let go of the past is to let yourself feel the pain around it. When you feel it, you can heal it.

You might feel sad about something that happened in the past, such as fighting with a friend. You might **regret** something that you did. However, you can't change the past. Becoming stuck in the past is not helpful for moving forward. Mindfulness helps you let go of the past and live in the present.

YOU MAY HAVE GONE THROUGH SOMETHING REALLY HARD IN YOUR PAST. YOU MIGHT NEED **THERAPY** TO LET IT GO.

# Focused on the Future

Focusing on the future also makes it hard to live your day-to-day life. It can cause a lot of **anxiety**. You may worry about a big test, game, event, or move that's coming up. You may worry that if you don't do everything right, you will lose what's important to you.

The truth is, you can't fix anything in the future. You can't know what will happen. You have no control over it. All you can control is the present.

COPING TOOLBOX

You might feel anxiety in your body: a racing heart, fast breathing, stomachache, and light-headedness.

Worrying about the future may make it hard to do anything at all. It puts a lot of **PRESSURE** on you.

9

Welcome to the Present!

If you can't live in the past or future, where can you live? In the present! That's what's happening right this moment. You may have no control over what happened or what will happen, but you can control how you **react** to what *is* happening.

For example, imagine that it's the night before a big **competition**. Your mind is running with thoughts: *I messed up last time. I'm going to mess up again.* You can use mindfulness—connecting to the present moment—to find your peace.

COPING TOOLBOX

MINDFULNESS WAS PRACTICED IN **ANCIENT** INDIA. MINDFULNESS IS IMPORTANT IN YOGA AND MEDITATION.

To relax into the present moment, you can say to yourself, "In this moment, I am okay."

11

♡ Take a Breath

The most important tool in your mindfulness toolbox is your breath. It can connect you to the present moment. You take it with you everywhere you go!

FIVE-FINGER BREATHING ALLOWS YOU TO PRACTICE FIVE FULL, DEEP, MINDFUL BREATHS.

COPING TOOLBOX

♡

ONE EXERCISE IS FIVE-FINGER BREATHING. PUT YOUR HAND OUT. TRACE UP EACH FINGER ON YOUR INHALE AND DOWN BETWEEN YOUR FINGERS ON EACH EXHALE.

First, become aware of your inhale (in breath) and exhale (out breath). That's one breath cycle. Just observe, or notice, your breath without judgment. How does it feel to breathe in and out? Is your breath fast or slow? It is deep or **shallow**? Try to take slow, deep breaths. Count at least five full breath cycles.

♡ Use Your Senses

Most people have five main senses. You can see, feel, hear, smell, and taste. You can use your senses to connect you to the present. This is called grounding.

One grounding exercise is called 5-4-3-2-1. First, look around you and name five things that you see. Then bring your focus to your body and name four things that you feel. Now listen for three things, such as a bird call or the wind. Name two things you can smell. Lastly, name one thing you can taste.

COPING TOOLBOX ♡

THINK ABOUT HOW YOUR BODY FEELS WHERE IT CONNECTS TO THE GROUND. DOES GRASS TICKLE YOUR ANKLES? ARE YOU SITTING ON A SOFT PILLOW?

Using your senses to connect to a moment can help you enjoy the moment too!

15

Only Observe

You can also practice mindfulness through meditation. In meditation, you "tune out" what's happening outside and "tune in" to what's happening inside. You start to build focus and slow down your thoughts.

To get started, find a quiet place to sit or lie down. Close your eyes. Then, start to observe your thoughts and **sensations** in the body. Don't judge them as good or bad. Only observe them as they come and go. You can name them simply: *hearing, feeling, thinking*.

COPING TOOLBOX

Meditation has roots in ancient India. Meditation based on observing what comes up in the mind and body is called *Vipassana*.

You can be curious about your thoughts and sensations. Your belly may rumble. You might have a song in your head. Let it all pass.

17

at Home in Your Body

Connecting to your body can help you feel grounded in the present. You can do this through sitting meditation. Just notice what you feel in your body. Do you have an itch on your elbow? Do you feel the wind in your hair?

Another way to connect mind to body is through movement. People do yoga poses to connect their mind and body. People also do walking meditation. To do this, walk very slowly and mindfully. Notice every movement and sensation as you walk.

COPING TOOLBOX

You can do a body scan to connect to your body. Lie down on the ground. Bring awareness to each body part and let go of any stress there.

This is called child's pose in yoga. Come to your hands and knees, then push your hips back. What do you feel in your body?

19

♡ Just Be

Mindfulness means knowing that you are exactly where you are supposed to be. You can't fix the past or control the future. All you can do is choose how to act right now.

You can do mindfulness exercises to invite yourself back to the present. Breathing, mindful movements, and grounding can open you up to this moment. It can change the way your brain works, allowing it to cope with stressful things. Then, you don't have to fight your stress anymore. You can just *be*.

COPING TOOLBOX

♡

YOU CAN EAT MINDFULLY TOO. HOLD YOUR FAVORITE FRUIT, OBSERVE IT, THEN EAT IT SLOWLY. TASTING YOUR FOOD BRINGS YOU INTO THE PRESENT!

PRACTICING MINDFULNESS CAN HELP REGULATE YOUR EMOTIONS, OR DEAL WITH YOUR FEELINGS IN A POSITIVE WAY.

21

GLOSSARY

ancient: Having to do with something or someone from long ago.

anxiety: A feeling of being worried or afraid something will happen.

competition: An event in which people try to win.

focus: Directed attention.

pressure: A force that pushes on something else.

react: To do something because something else happens.

regret: To feel sorry for something you did.

sensation: Something that you feel.

shallow: Not deep.

stress: Something that causes strong feelings of worry.

therapy: A method used to treat a problem in the body or mind.

FOR MORE INFORMATION

BOOKS

Alladin, Erin. *A World of Mindfulness.* Ontario, Canada: Pajama Press, 2020.

Kinder, Wynne. *Calm: Mindfulness for Kids.* New York, NY: DK Publishing, 2019.

Willard, Christopher. *Alphabreaths: The ABCs of Mindful Breathing.* Boulder, CO: Sounds True, 2022.

WEBSITES

Coping Skill Spotlight: 5 4 3 2 1 Grounding Technique
copingskillsforkids.com/blog/2016/4/27/coping-skill-spotlight-5-4-3-2-1-grounding-technique
Learn how to do 5-4-3-2-1 grounding to help you cope with hard feelings.

Mindfulness
kidshealth.org/en/kids/mindfulness.html#catpeople
Explore more about mindfulness with KidsHealth.

Mindfulness Exercises
kidshealth.org/en/kids/mindful-exercises.html#catpeople
Try different mindfulness exercises such as mindful eating and breathing.

INDEX